APJ Abdul Kalam —The Missile Man of India

Dr. APJ Abdul Kalam is one of the most distinguished scientist of India. He is a renowned professor, aeronautical engineer and the chancellor of the Indian Institute of Space Science and Technology (IIST).

Dr. APJ Abdul Kalam served as the 11th President of India from 2002 to 2007. He is often referred as 'People's President'. He is also popularly known as the 'Missile Man of India', because of his extraordinary contribution in the development of Ballistic Missile project and Space Rocket Technology. He also worked as a scientist in ISRO and DRDO. He was awarded with the Bharat Ratna—India's highest civilian honour in 1997.

Birth and Early Years of Dr. Kalam's Life

Dr. APJ Abdul Kalam was born in Rameshwaram (in Tamilnadu) in a middle-class Muslim family on 15th October 1931. His father was Jainulabdeen and mother was Ashiamma. Dr. Kalam's full name is Avul Pakir Jainulabdeen. His father was a devout Muslim, who had good relations with the Rameshwaram temple priests. He used to rent his owned boats out to the local fishermen. He was a good friend of the Hindu religious leaders and school teachers of Rameshwaram.

During his childhood, Dr. Kalam lived very close to the sea. He developed a great passion for nature and sea. He used to spend a lot of time watching the waves of sea. His mother influenced him to a great extent in developing his talents in music and writing poetry.

Dr. Kalam's parents led a very simple lifestyle. They imbibed good moral values in their children. Dr. Kalam became religious at a very young age. He reads 'Quran' and 'Bhagwat Geeta' daily and strictly follows vegetarian diet. Dr. Kalam devoted his entire life in doing research work.

Dr. Kalam spent most of his childhood in financial problems. His education began in a rural primary school at Rameshwaram. Later, he was shifted to Ramnathpuram Missionary School.

Dr. Kalam started working at a very early age. To bear the expenses of his education, he worked as a newspaper hawker.

His teachers, parents and others noticed his efforts and brilliance. Some of his teachers even came forward to help him.

After completing his school education in 1954, he took his graduation degree in Physics from St. Joseph College, Tiruchirapalli. In 1957, Kalam completed Bachelor of Engg. in Aerospace engineering from Madras Institute of Technology. Later he obtained advanced master and doctorate degrees in his respected field from the same institute.

Dr. Kalam's Professional Life

After completing his third year at MIT, he joined Hindustan Aeronautics Limited (HAL), Bangalore as a trainee and worked on the piston and turbine engines. In 1958, he came out of Hindustan Aeronautics Limited as a graduate.

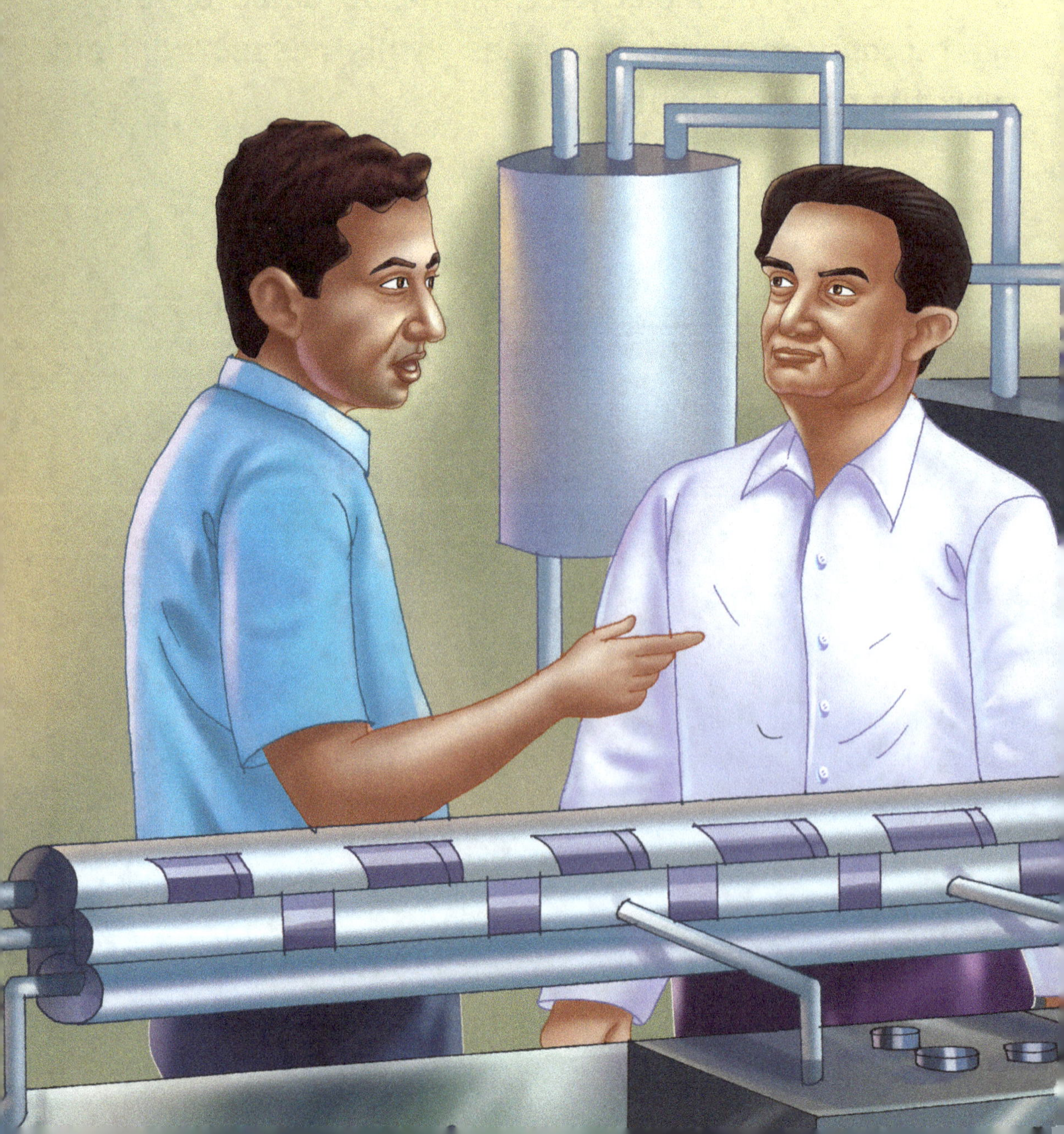

Thereafter, he got the opportunity to sewed at Indian Space Research Organisation (ISRO). After working on the several projects, he soon became a Project Director for India's first indigenous satellite launch vehicle (SLV-III) at Thumba.

The SLV-3 project was successful in placing Rohini—a scientific satellite—into orbit in July 1980 and was honoured with a Padma Bhushan in 1981. During this time, Dr. Kalam got to work with three great minds—Dr. Vikram Sarabhai, Professor Satish Dhawan and Dr. Brahm Prakash. He has also acknowledged these three people in his autobiography.

The second phase of Dr. Kalam's professional life started when he joined Defence Research Development Organisation (DRDO) in 1982. As Director of DRDO, he was entrusted with Integrated Guided Missile Development Program (IGMDP).

He played a major role in the development of many important Missiles like Nag, Akash, Trishul, Agni and Prithvi.

Three new laboratories for missile technologies were also developed during his tenure. His contributions in India's defence system are admirable.

Thereafter, Dr. Kalam worked as the Chairman of the Technology, Information, Forecasting and Assessment Council (TIFAC).

Dr. Kalam played a significant role in India's Pokharan-II nuclear test that was conducted in 1998.

In November 1999, Dr. Kalam was appointed as the Chief Scientific Advisor to the Govt. of India.
Later, in November 2001 he Joined Anna University at Chennai as a Professor of Technology and Societal Transformation.

Dr. Kalam—A Great Leader

When Dr. Kalam was working at the Rocket launching station in Thumba, there were around 70 scientists working under his leadership. To get success in their work and plan the scientists used to work for 12 to 18 hours daily. They could hardly spare any time for their families.

One day, a scientist came to Dr. Kalam and said, "Sir, I've promised my kids to take them to the exhibition going on in the town. So, I want to leave at 5.30 pm today, if you permit."

Dr. Kalam accepted his request and permitted him to leave at 5.30 pm. The scientist got engaged in his work. But when he finished the work it was almost 8.00 pm. He felt very bad that he had broken the promise given to his kids. Dr. Kalam was not in the office at that time.

In a Sad and tired mood, when he reached home he saw that his children were not at home. He asked to his wife about them. She replied, "Your Boss came here around 5.00 pm and took our kids for the exhibition."

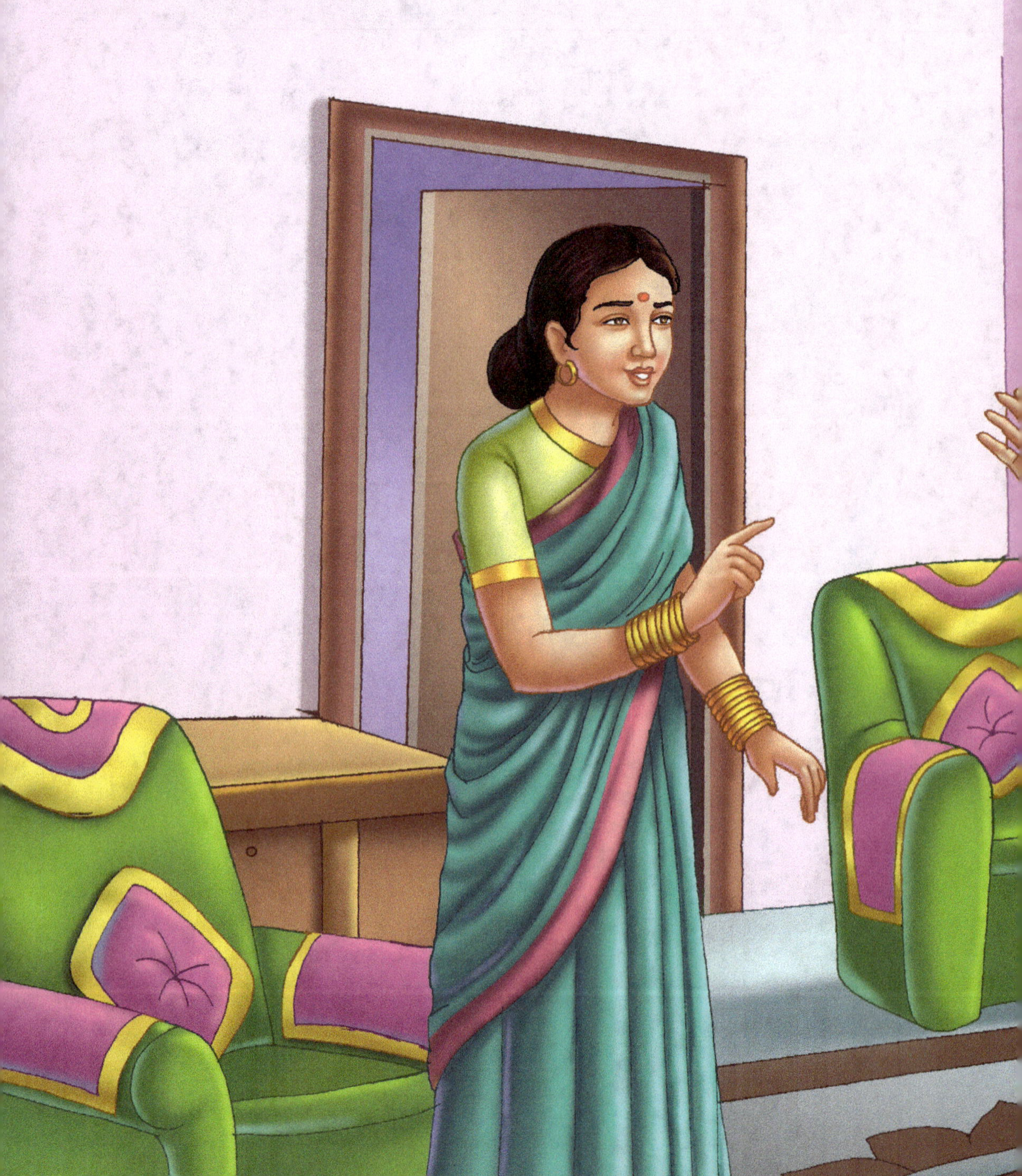

The scientist was overwhelmed by the sweet gesture of his boss. Actually, Dr. Kalam saw that the scientist was engrossed in a very important work. And, he didn't want to disappoint the kids. So, he decided to take his children on his behalf for the exhibition.

Such an understanding and caring boss was Dr. Kalam.

Dr. Kalam as the President of India

The entire nation was surprised when the ruling NDA Government nominated Dr. Kalam—the famous scientist—as their candidate for the President elections. He won the election by huge margin and became the 11th President of India on 25th July 2002.

In his speech during the oath taking ceremony, Dr. Kalam said that we should be proud of our country, "In the last 50 years, India has made many achievements in the fields of food production, health sector, higher education, media & mass communication, information technology, science and defence. In spite of these advancements, a large population is still struggling with the problems like poverty, unemployment, diseases and lack of education."

Dr. Kalam expressed his vision to eradicate all the problems from the country and making it the strongest nation one day.

During his tenure, Dr. Kalam worked especially in the fields of science and education. He was remained as an approachable and humble President. He is very fond of the children and is always concerned for their development and welfare. He aimed to make India a scientifically strong nation and always tries to ignite the spark in the minds of Indian citizens.

Dr. Kalam has a multifaceted personality. Apart from being a great scientist, he is also interested in the field of arts and culture. He has written many books including his autobiography, 'Wings of Fire'. Some of his famous books are: 'Scientist to President', 'Ignited Minds: Unleashing the Power Within India', 'India 2020' etc.

He has also written Tamil poetry. Dr. Kalam is good at playing the Indian musical instrument 'Veena'.

Dr. Kalam has three visions. His first vision is freedom. He said that our country was ruled by many and remained dependent for a long period but we the Indians respect other's freedom, thus India has great values and culture.

Dr. Kalam's second vision is development. He said that though we have achieved a lot in the last few years, but we need to have more development, especially in the fields of education, science and technology.

His third vision is that India must be strong and emerge as a super power. It should stand up to the world and show its strength.

Dr. Kalam wants to make India an advanced and technologically developed nation. In his book, 'India 2020', he has mentioned an action plan to make India a knowledge superpower and a developed nation by the year 2020.

Dr. Kalam has been awarded with Bharat Ratna (1997), Padma Vibhushan (1990), Padma Bhushan (1981) and also received many more prestigious honours and awards.

He is presently the Chancellor of the Indian Institute of Space and Technology and also works as a professor at Anna University (Chennai) and as a visiting faculty in many academic and research institutes through out the country.

In May 2011, Dr. Kalam started a new mission for the Indian youth. 'What Can I Give Movement', is a unique mission to inculcate the Universal spirit of giving in the youth.

For years, Dr. Kalam has been inspiring many lives, especially the youth and children. He is the ocean of knowledge. We should draw inspiration from his life and must work to make India- a strongest nation.

On July 27, 2015, Dr. Kalam died after collapsing, while delivering a lecture at IIM, Shillong, Meghalaya. He was 83. The whole Nation mourned on his death, and paid homage, includes the President, the PM and other dignitaries, to him.

Chanakya—The Pioneer Economist of India

Chanakya is one of the greatest personalities of Indian history. He was the advisor and Prime Minister to the Emperor, Chandragupta Maurya. He was a professor at the University of Takshila and was well known for his expertise in Commerce, Economics and various other subjects.

Chanakya is also known as Kautilya and Vishnugupta Sharma. He was born in 370 BC. He has been honoured by the title of the 'Pioneer Economist of India'. He authored two ancient Indian treatises named 'Arthashastra' and 'Neetishastra'.

With the help of Chandragupta Maurya, Chanakya established the Mauryan Dynasty after defeating the Nanda kings.

Birth and Early Years of Chanakya's Life

Chanakya was born in a Brahmin family in 370 BC, in the city of Patliputra (Patna), Bihar. His father was Acharya Chanak, who being a teacher wanted to provide the best education to Chanakya.

Chanakya received his education at Takshashila (Taxila)—the ancient centre for culture and education. At a very young age, he had memorised the Vedas, which were considered as the toughest scriptures.

Since childhood, Chanakya was inclined towards political study too. His extraordinary wisdom and tact were evident in his nature. His second interest was Economics. He studied and gained expertise in Economics as well.

After completing his education, Chanakya started teaching at Takshashila (Taxila). He believed in sharing education and knowledge with others, so that they could also be benefited by it.

Chanakya proved to be an ideal teacher. He imparted education to his students in a interactive and practical way and hence became a popular and respected teacher of his times. His students came from royal families which enabled Chanakya to know most of the political happenings in the country.

Chanakya once came to know that there were chances of foreign invasion in India. Europe's great warrior Salukes was preparing his armies to attack India. On the other hand, the ruler of Patliputra, Dhanananda was torturing the people of the kingdom. The neighbouring countries were also ready to invade the weak areas of India.

Understanding the internal and the external situation, Chanakya decided to leave the University and do something to save the nation. With this thought in his mind, he left Takshashila and moved to Patliputra.

Chanakya in Patliputra

Patliputra (presently known as Patna) was a prosperous city famous for its rich culture. It was also a business centre. Since most essential commodities were produced in the city. Patliputra always welcomed scholars and artists. Chanakya reached the city and started his first campaign from here. The ruler of Patliputra, Dhananada was a cruel king. Who used to collect heavy taxes from the people of his kingdom, to accumlate wealth.
Chanakya was sad on witnessing the condition at Patliputra. He joined a committee made by the king for charity purposes.

The committee, called Sungha (Trust), was headed by scholars and the influential people of the city. Chanakya was later appointed as the President of the Sungha (Trust).

As the President of the trust, Chanakya used to meet King Dhanananda several times. Unlike other courtiers, Chanakya never tried to flatter the king. He was always very clear and straightforward in his communication with the king.

The king didn't like the rude and harsh behaviour of Chanakya. He removed him from the position of the President without any reason. Chanakya became very angry on this.

The king ordered his soldiers to throw Chanakya out of the palace. While his soldiers were pushing Chanakya out of the court, the knot of his hair got opened. Chanakya felt highly insulted. He vowed not to tie the knot of his hair till he puts one ends to the entire Nanda dynasty.

Chanakya Meets Chandragupta

Walking on the streets of Patliputra angrily, he stumbled upon a stump of grass. He decided to went out his anger in the right way. He sat down and started plucking the strands of grass.

While Chanakya was busy plucking grass, he saw some young boys playing in the ground. One of the boys was acting like a king and others as his courtiers and people. The boys who were acting like the people of kingdom came forward one by one with their problems. And, the boy acting as the king gave solutions to each and every problem.

Chanakya was highly impressed by the intelligence and righteousness of the boy. He approached the boy and asked him, "Who are you?"

"Sir, my name is Chandragupta," replied the young boy. Chandragupta told Chanakya everything about his life and his family background.

He said, "Sir, Nandas killed my father and brothers. Now, I want to take revenge from them."

King Dhananada was also a Nanda king and Chanakya wanted to take a revenge from him. Since, he joined hands with Chandragupta. He vowed to destroy the Nanda king and promised the throne of Patliputra to Chandragupta.

Great Works of Chanakya

While carrying out the responsibilities of the Magadh Empire, Chanakya started penning down his great work. He wrote the treatise on politics and administration—Arthashastra. The book discusses monetary policies, welfare and international strategies and warfare in detail. This book became popular worldwide and was later translated in many Indian and European languages.

Another book written by Chanakya was 'Neetishastra' or 'Chanakya Neeti'. It is the treatise on the ideal way of life. Chanakya also wrote 'Neetisutras' (aphorisms). Out of these 455 sutras, about 216 are on rajneeti (politics) to guide the kings and administrators.

Among his various contributions to the nation, his role in establishing the Mauryan Empire is the most praiseworthy.

Last Years of Chanakya's Life

According to a popular legend, Chanakya started adding poison in the food of King Chandragupta Maurya to make his body immune to the effects of poison. Since during that time it was common practise to kill the kings by giving poision.

Chanakya had no ill intention in giving poison to the king. But one day, by mistake, King's wife-Queen Durdhara who was pregnent, shared the food with the king. When Chanakya came to know about this, he got worried for the baby.

He immediately operated the queen and took the baby out safely. Unfortunately, the queen died because of effects of poison. The prince was named as Bindusara.

When Bindusara entered his youth, Chandragupta Maurya gave the throne to him. He retired from his duties to spend rest of his life in meditation. He went to a place called Shravana Belagola in Karnataka, and lived there till the end of his life.

On the other hand, Chanakya continued to be the Prime Minister and advisor to Bindusara. One of the other ministers of Bindusara named Subandhu didn't like Chanakya. Once, he told Bindusara that Chanakya was responsible for his mother's death. Bindusara believed Subandhu and decided to take revenge.

When Chanakya came to know about the incident, he decided to end his life. He renounced everything, distributed his wealth among the poor and needy, abstained from food and water and sat for deep meditation.

Meanwhile, Bindusara came to know about the complete story of his birth through his nurses. He also came to know that Chanakya was the one who saved his life. He rushed to Chanakya to apologise. But Chanakya didn't change his mind. In 283 BC, at the age of 87, great Chanakya died.

Bindusara repented for his actions badly. He blamed Subandhu for misguiding him. Chanakya's death was the greatest loss not only for Bindusara but also for the entire nation.

Chanakya has been a great inspiration and a role model for many kings and administrators. His knowledge and understanding of the politics and economics was beyond admiration. His theories gave a new shape and system to our nation.

Chanakya's contribution to the Indian history and society as a whole is extraordinary. His life proves that with a strong determination, anyone can achieve anything.